THE WAYFARER

The Wayfarer

MEERA CHAKRAVORTY

PARTRIDGE

A Penguin Company

Partridge books may be ordered through booksellers or by contacting:

Partridge India
Penguin Books India Pvt.Ltd
11, Community Centre, Panchsheel Park, New Delhi 110017
India
www.partridgepublishing.com
Phone: 000.800.10062.62

CONTENTS

Dedicated to Earth

The Author of Clothes

The dress had to be arresting
she knew
people are passionate about their appearances
she was searching for perfection
like a song of an opera
caring deeply what she designed
making it fit for the thin vase-body
a key text of semeiology . . .

There appeared the high priestesses
from the fashion world of Paris
their glory-days
reflected on their pride
their adoration far-reaching.
In an act of ironic resistance
they explored
wearing a frivolous smile

breaking through the sky.

She stood there all alone . . .

When the dress let itself go
over the author of clothes
it had finally enabled
a celebration of being humane.

To Tagore

Lest my unfinished melody
I fear
come in your way
with it's impertinent intrusion
may I take your leave for a little reverie—

Your faultless melody
touched me profoundly
the joy of which
I have celebrated over the ages
carried it to the hill's silence.

I shall now
not in a vain attempt though
beseech you
to breath fresh life
into my ever erring flute
to fill it
with joy unrestrained
for my little indulgence.

The Age of 3 Pretence

The time that you soften your voice
is the time you take so long.
With affected surprise
and pleasing countenance
you seek to emphasize
each word of pleasantry
adding a sort of mysteriousness.

You presume
to be the cause of all causes
of time and beyond . . .
with delightful habit of knocking
at my alien door
you promise to take my chariot
through the wilderness of the world
hoping to offer the price of my deliverance
on your hollow platter.

Meltdown

Their elliptic dances
brought drought
desertification
shocking disaster to peoples' wealth
led them to the road
to unknown darkness
with emptiness
staring at them ceaselessly.

Now . . .
after the party is over
there begins the excavation
of the cause and effect
through the seemingly bloodless debris
to the Wall street collapse
while the other glorious responses
remain unmindful
of the bodies
that emerge from the wreckage.

5
The Tree Husband

They never noticed her except when they wanted to
she was shy and tranquil
like the receding wave that carries sand with it.
She carried entrusted shadows
from the night's unerring constellations
from the hush in the Oceanside house
tinkering with the freedom of the wind
her house of childhood.

She did not have a dancer's legs
neither fair skin nor titillating talks
yet, she could dance on waves
even on very cold nights.
She fiddled the dry leaves
longed for wordless song
to gift to the mango blossom
to the berry bushes her smile and charm.

The evening wind reminded her of the tree
she cared for
when she stood before him
watched his adoring color
incapable of indifference towards her
watched the festival of leaves
that long prevailed across the grass
the shady dance floor.

Despite her simplicity
they did not like her.

Faces behind faces
talked about her crazy discords
her family-murmurs
her fumbling groans.
They called her
a lingering vile shadow
they would like to avoid forever
this deaf and dumb dirt.
But who would marry her
this nightmare
perilous for a family!

So . . .
they got her married to the tree
the whole village
witnessed this.
She loved her tree-husband
adorned it's stem
with garlands of flowers
cleaned the garbage at its foot
that came with the rain water.
Her tree-husband huge in stature
she knew his gruffness
felt his generous gaze though.

MEERA CHAKRAVORTY

Once, when the night was terrifying
two men got together
walked to a neighbor hood bar
'the good and the evil are the destinies you can't change'
yelled one of them
the residue from the bottle
making a thin crooked curve on his chin:
'this girl is evil,
the dumb girl,
I have thought of a plan'.
There was a thrill
in his raucous voice
deeply watchful, the other listened.
They debated her death
by waylaying her.
However, the first of the rigid vipers
had an icy idea.
'You will have a roller coaster-excitement
when you listen to my plan,
drink your glass now, you fool'
he screamed.

That stormy night they grabbed her
turned her around to tie her to the tree
the groaning in her throat, they knew
no one will hear
no one will hear her fumbling
not even their whooping laughter
in this night of terrible storm and lightening.

The more the storm became ferocious,
more frenzy they got.
The wind finally unbuckled itself
turned dangerously wicked
twisted the uneven branches
hit the men
slapping them with thunderous force
pushing them to the stem of the huge tree.
They fell with a thud
yet another branch curved upon them
hoisting their bodies up
throwing them back to the garbage
collected underneath.

By the time the wind withdrew
the men lay dead.

Frightened, yet amazed, she watched
the tranquility of his shade
her tree-husband had brought to her
the tender peace,
she wondered about his self-contained grace
over the years she had only adored.
Now,
she felt a strange emotion
that did not go unnoticed
the serenity
in her dark loving eyes.
and love
in the depth of her own heart.

MEERA CHAKRAVORTY

May I have a Corner in Your Garden

The Spring ushered me in her garden
leaving in a hurry
apologized that there was no other better person
than me to keep her treasure with.
I already have enough things to linger on . . .
where could I possibly keep
her futile leaves and abandoned flowers
spread by the frivolous wind.

May I have a corner in your garden
to store the clamorous, the despaired, deserted rainbow
that she left behind
or hope
that
she will be back
mounting the languid hours
to take care of her flowers
she had grown
with no more gaze of emptiness.

Time Drowns Itself

Every year the earth cries for silver waves
lamenting emptiness.
His meghamalhar fails to bathe
the sky anymore
the thousand-eyed one
people worship him
for the reason he is not aware of
the rise in stock market
while the paddy dances to fearful tunes
aghast by the acres of poppies
going to blossom soon . . .
If this is your moment to shine
so be it.

I stop
beside my little piece of sky
pale through the window
allow me to hear the resonance of rains
unmindful of the household work
I watch the festival of Shravana.
The fractured rain-clouds
reminds Parthasarathy's refusal
to help the haughty ones any more.

This is how
the time drowns itself
into it's own endless waves.
ceaselessly
rider-less.

The Show

You take flowers from the bunch
make them vanish in thin air
bring in a pair of pigeons.
Whirling your red scarf
cut the body of a damsel into two,
she comes back dancing joyously
your show a fabulous success.

You turn to the whimsical breeze
make it run miles together
to chase the starry eyed shadow
crush the soundless breath
you choke the silence of the night
holding her against your chest
with no love to enchant her.

She drops down through the darkness
never to come back
dancing smilingly.
You hold the silver coin
that will not pierce the wind
to vanish in the night-veiled sky
but will remain over your grave for ever
as a moment of grief.

The Mountain Daughter

Folks cheering Parvati loudly
they remind her
it is her day
hill-walking, their cheers resonate.

Parvati, the mountain-daughter
from the Himalayan terrain
woke up hearing a sudden thud
blowing her door
getting quicker and louder every moment,
people crowded at the stone-steps
screamed, hurry Parvati,
the bear has taken away the little Loku.

She ran,
a race against time
with people behind her
beating drums and vessels.
She ran into mountain's boudoir
the beast stomped it's feet in anger
leaped forward with rage
to pounce on her
wrestling with air
a lightening-moment . . .

Parvati's spear tossed it down.
A rugged silence followed
the folks watched holding their breath
Loku crawling from the cave
the sun hung in the mid air.
Cheering with joy
the people shouted, Parvati, its your day,
let's celebrate.

Cheers squeezed swiftly through
the mountain caves
whispers lingered with unexplained joy.
Parvati walked along the stream
loads of woods on her head
slowly
welcoming her self-assuring tears
she walked alone
waving at the invisible stars
under the Autumn-sky.

Uneasy Tranquil

The noise and the smoke
cover the sky with insomnia
Sun lights the hazy horizon
hand-crafted it's fringes.
Birds, happy to travel
now remain silent
long to play with clouds though.
The river flows drowsily
through dust and darkness
on the bank stands the hollow taverns and cafes
with shadows of apocalypse frightening the poor rustic town.

The Vanity Song

The edge of your mid-day fire
does not injure their thick skins.
To defy you
they shut themselves up in the destitute conversations
their insipid pages of lives
filled with dissipation
decry people crushed on the roads.
Drunk with pride
they run from sky to sky
wail vanity songs in chorus
wish to call you a friend
when face to face with death
never to rue it in tears.

Ineffable

Once when there were whispers
that you are coming
the little flute had sung
endless melodies to me
I shower them on you today
to bring you joy ineffable.

In this Land of Indifference:
An Ode to Gandhi

I had heard about you from father
you were in the thick of the movement
dragged by the denser and darker nights
with the burden of dependence on
the white men
over your shoulder.

You were split
running between home and world
urging people to leave
the saddle of the British-raj
allowing the destitute seasons to
take care of you endlessly
dreaming of the oncoming freedom
which the mighty songs of prisons
promised
you embraced their barracks
as one embraces timid friends
beaten by the whirl wind
you shunned violence
refused to lead
a blood-reddened earth
yet
took the voyage destroying blind alleys.

As your picture is placed on this wall
and on the other
they come and ask
'who is he'?
Some of those who know you
answer with silence
others with negative pride . . .

In this land of indifference
on the naked crushed roads
you stand there smiling
at those
who do not like to sing
the songs of your victory.

For the First Shower of August

That happy moment has come again
when the drizzles had signaled
your arrival
with eyes shinning in freedom
your unbound joy
made the passing breeze filled with whisper
gave me your signature of love
on many skies.

A Portrait of Fog

The December fog stood silent
between the buildings.
Emily wanted to embrace it joyfully
tumbling clownishly on my bed
she said gaily
Wow, what a nice day!

I stared through the dull glass of the window
the berry bushes had disappeared
in the wild of the fog
I had an invitation to the Indo-French festival
wondered how would I reach
a little wave of quietness
mocked my futile enthusiasm
the leisurely sunlight would not stir
the still leaves for sometime now
I felt I did not exist.

How strange to think of my non-existence
not by death
but by fading out in the fog . . . .

16 A Part-time Gardner

In the mahagony woods
I waited day long
unsupported by the foliage
I waited to linger on
to the silence of the winter-sun
the wind was pre-occupied
clamorous and slippery in my company
half way along the forest it hurried off
like a crazy pedestrian
with savage-signs to stop the bus
heading towards the children's school.

Lounging in the woods
I gazed upon the cold December morning
of arbitrary date
did I hear the passing seconds
fiddling with the notes of a song
coming from the Bays water
way back home
I asked myself
in exchange of what
would I like to be here
a part-time Gardner.

And so said Sita . . .

Don't apologize alarmingly, Lakshmana
don't say what he had been thinking all day
or
that he had been troubled
his silence
that's all that matters to me.

How did he send me to wander off
around the moors
surely
the king's folly
cannot see through the frozen darkness
his love-oaths made only to be broken
when,
tenderly glancing at me
he had made me feel at home in high heavens!
Oh, how this silence
ceased my breath.

But, not any more, Lakshmana,
now the earth has sent me
her love
I will not be homeless again.
Winds are cold but not mourning
I am indeed returning to my home
to earth's cradle of blue lakes
with her many songs of seasons
to her swift running rivers
with whom I will weave my words
tomorrow will not be bitter morning, Lakshmana,
your king's razor-edged silence
will no more leave
earth and me alone.

18

I Walk Past . . .

I walk past the Gulmohars
aligned on a narrow road
that used to be emptier
mystifying—
Well, that was then . . .

Now, when I drift off boldly
I see the flowers soberly poised
at the threshold of my garden
urging me for a re-acquaintance
not knowing that it is I
who wanted to see them again
like the evening Purabi-ambience
rising and gliding
like a waking dream.

Self-possessed, the Gulmohars wait
for a long time since the last spring
for the road to have
no more traumatic boughs
to welcome the joy of the unbound birds
curving from peak to peak
acknowledging the credit for their fine performance.

Whirled Up

The anguished silence of your eyes
makes me a fugitive
I am gripped with a compelling wish
for a few minutes to sail with the east-wind
the wood-loads are unhinged and uncertain
so am I
betrayed by my dormant memories
I wish I do not fall deep into
an un-giving conversation
to re-involve my futile journey with yours.

Words

Bewitching is your love
with colors intently imbued
like the rainbow-archway
pursuing it's voyage
with ecstasy born of Cupid . . . .

You want me to address these words to you.

I sigh—
not from happiness
but from surprise at your way of saying
I don't repeat imaginary words
as you do
words like, I love you . . .
they stare at me
blunt and lonely
stop abruptly at the frontiers of my heart
as if they could never bear to
leave them to themselves . . .
Unmindful I move
into the dusk
into the night's song
waiting for love to give itself to me
with silent tenderness.

Meera Chakravorty

Shelter I did not Ask

With the restless wind
I walked around with no aim
I had snatched the day from the sky
to be with you
when my life was not half gone
I wanted to be with you.

You looked at your busy schedules
they were a template of market products
scribbled over the back of my letters I wrote
during long rainy hours
never ever read
they remained unshared
scattered on the floor . . .

Drizzles of light
trying to get through the crack of the window
I keep gazing—
Has the weather gone awry
why am I waiting so long
half loved
behind this timid door
for the shelter I didn't ask.
Before the day light merges
with the chilling black night
I will go to the blue Aparajitas
now in bloom
once again for their love-touch.

The Unstated

22

You walked down the path
to the far away station
heedless of the insistent traffic passing
through the Central park
I remained to listen to the hushed song
of the Bays water
thinking of your eluding move.

What moved you to this strange action
I know not
but I would like to see you
I owe it to you
to your subservience of love.

On that April morning
I remember
you stood there ahead of me
for a moment
neither you moved nor I
then for some reason pretty uncertain
you whispered warmly
backed up by your sacred honor
as you paused before the silent mist
I could gather your words
my most valued possession
though unstated.

...For the Next Spring

Did you see the dark panic in me
with color less deeper
with smell fainter.
Your upbringing
uniquely different from mine
color so deep
fragrance so unreachable
you took me to the world of art
the world which was opaque to me earlier
held me with a touch of gentleness
you walked along with me to the fair.

As the fair closed
You opened your door
reassured, I stop by your flower garden
longing for the next spring.

Obeisance to Sister Nivedita

In the busy moments of my music
I felt self-possessed
the tide of people
bursting forth to their leader
made me feel stranger than we are
I felt exalted but dizzy
may be lack of air
may be proximity to the crowd.
But when I chanced upon you
on the translucent horizon
how entranced I had been
by your portrait
your promised touch
ignoring the long cherished hours
swayed by the restless luminous Beethoven
you impelled me to be aware of
yet another presence
in my music.

Covered with the Golden Disc

Through winter into spring
the Sun with his aching passion
ignored the bleakness in my mind
I planned to stay here I said
for the sake of love
outside your door all alone
it would be unbearable betrayal on my part
my reeling spirit
to leave without seeing you.
I coaxed you into courage
followed you like a phantom
my being completely foreshadowed by yours
I asked you to uncover the golden disk
after which I said I would depart in silence
yet survive in your light.

The Raison d'etre

The dear husband of my dear daughter
in fact my dear son-in-law
never heedless nor guilty of omissions generally
an agreeable gentleman
serious as Marx
honored me recently by offering his
prestigious card
with it's virtual existence though
this is for your security reference, he explained
you may show it in the airport on demand.
Friends unaware
frowned in disappointment
you borrowing fool
they cried out
trying to explore my purse to the extreme far edge
I laughed my heart out
reassured them
that I am no borrower
that I was only telling the half-truth.

Snubbed by their contemptuous look
I explained
how my son-n-law had to process the air ticket
for my trip to Delhi
which required a copy of his credit-card as an evidence
if demanded.

Well, in my dreams
I do not rule out using his card
for a trip to Paris sometime
but for that
there has to be a divine interference
to execute this wish
explaining the raison d'etre.

Nachikatas and Mark Zuckerberg

Yama, the Hindu god of death-darkness
offered Nachiketas, the sage-son
three boons to opt to
go beyond darkness
to the world of magic-joy
of glowing cheeks.
By the first boon, he said,
you can be Mark Zuckerberg
bringing security to your paternal family
by the second, Cleopatra and Liz Taylors
embrace them with open arms
do not worry about the descending slopes.

Ah yes! Said Nachiketas,
these your boons are
as morbid as your dark region
your wealth has a blank future Yama
with money-barons gasping to erase
Occupy Wall Streets.

Mark my words
even for Zuckerberg
these were no nocturnal rituals
stuck below the glowing cheeks.
All this can never take me to the region
beyond darkness
nor hide any one from your ceaseless
deathly world of god-fathers.

Grant me the third boon Yama
by which I will choose the moon
unmindful of it's borrowed light
always absent for half a month
yet
cool, soothing and undeathly.

28

The River-Narrative

The river flows
shore-less for quite long
then
comes down further
shrinks gradually
entering the woods through the village
invites them to
listen to her melodies
her strange verses—

The woods
harsh and dissonant
breaks into vain shrill
with eyes loveless and dark
wishes to spread it's insomnia
across the river . . . .

The village on the other side
with hollow restlessness
screams in a ghostly voice
wishes to crush the secretive woods to dust
finally,
purposeless and self-possessed
they do not allow the river-dialogue
her narrative
her paintings
the only tangible way
to enter their darkness
through their schizophrenia.

Cosmetic Love

The red Gulmohars
in their startling chorus
paint the sky-silk with April flames
some of them with unerring passion
stretch their tiny hands to
the bunch of flying envy-green parrots.

You stand before the modest grill
bound in your endless ego
pluck some of them
not to put them in your garland though
you pluck them with craftsmanship
without a touch of pain
your cosmetic love
unrestrained as always
never allows them to
drop in dust on their own.

Bring Fire Sahadeva!

A discarded invitee you are
aren't you
in this assembly, to play dice?
Roared Bheema, the second Pandava
not just to carry on the chess-game
but to checkmate
to provoke death
you, O discard,
wish to come here repeatedly
want to be the Grandmaster
though get defeated and doomed every time.

You Yudhishthira, the rogue-husband
you used Draupadi as the bait
and so
wanted to marry the hypnotically beautiful one
pretending
as the last romantic of the Victoria-version
wanted to make cover-girl out of her . . .
Drawing on the power of our mother's advice
you show-cased your talent your degradation
and remained altogether timid
unnamed, unrevealed
the visibly invisible stupid nincompoop
tried your best to project your dream image.

Ah, you already had in your mind
Draupadi as the stake
for raising funds for your gamble
a sort of slave-trading.
Despite repeated pleadings by Vidura
you stubbornly refused to decline the invitation to play dice
quite aware of the revelations of the vile secrets of Duryodhana though
willingly ignored his pragmatic voice.

But wait . . .
you pushed your luck too far
I have a dislike of the authorial signature
that you often flung.
Now, you are an absence of décor
of the royal insignia
your most vulnerable part, your sense of justice
ha! will now be torn apart.
Fie upon you,
aren't you called 'the dharma', the righteousness personified?
I will return it to you as brutally as possible.
Sahadeva, bring fire
burn his fingers
ever tempted to fondle the dice

I will continue with this fire-sacrifice
for no better reason than
using women as property
as stake
for which
Draupadi and many other women today
have descended into horror.

Eliminate these discarded rogues, Sahadeva,
bring fire!
the patience has withered away
burn these incurables
these contagious, grotesque irremediable
for whom
women are bait for ever
burn, burn these grave diggers
ah! How words fail me Sahadeva . . .
bring fire!
let it engulf these condemned souls
the failing barbarians
their forever unraveled disguises
which
continue to stop women everyday from existing.

For Aung San Suu Kyi

You have come through the darkness Suu Kyi
the old thinking will go
but not before it tries once again
to think
how to bring the tragic falling back.

These are the mean days
Yet,
the varied dreams
deliberate every time
allow some kind of continuity
for the poet to be
the ruptured palm leaves around the garden
expect to catch you sooner or later
with rains in hand
their nerveless sob
a kind of catharsis.

You are watched from the crooked Verandah
your care taker looks in vain.
Moonlight spills to the floor of your sketchy words.
His drowsy gaze
goes wrapped
in his own messy shadow
he pulls off some work-sheets
to write a complaint against you
that you have an atrocious handwriting
which goes one way or the other
but finds it's rhythm and creates a pattern
such that
he fails to find a message
he thinks you want to sent to an ally . . .
and so,
you must improve your writing Suu Kyi,
that has no magic in it
exploring the interesting nuances
to help him pick a message
from your poetry.

Expository

The road near this lake
in it's early days
was innocently straight forward
ran along with us carrying our bicycle rides
bumping into the village.
Cowherd boys sitting drowsily
under the burning mid-sun
sometimes running behind the leaflets dropped by
parties contesting election
at other times
playing cricket unglamorously.
The road
archived by the children's games
once in a while
enjoining an audience
remained ecstatic.

Then came the dreaded footsteps
as 'Experts'
with their soaked craft
to pattern many subways
'to link people'
as they said,
'with their survival'.

The villagers have been silent though
the woodpeckers, the mainas, and their friends
rushed to the taller light-posts
the only remaining substitutes
for building their nests on
their mourning songs
exploring
the absent longing of the dead trees
their childhood stream caving around
rhyming with their sonorous songs.

Over that distant arch
gathered a dense fabric-moments
moments that were curious
playful and vibrating
moments of showing off . . . .
With the arch now refigured
along with the road
all theses moments
have gone deep into the structure
to be rewritten by the soaked crafts
as they said—
'for the survival of people'!

Now,
the sunset notes of these birds
will forever be stuck
on the subway paintings
showing their pale photographs
with a message that says,
'they also have right to exist'.

The Writer

Quite indifferent to the writer
the books are by themselves
standing diligently before him nevertheless.
He sits there fearing their anachronism
thinking
they already might have felt foreign to him . . .
because,
he does not speak in their language
cannot talk to them about the Red-Indian landscape
or
proclaim his faith to them, his inner being.
In their world he has no work
or
may be, he has
for a distant purpose.
Yet,
they command him his presence
into the endless squares of the shelves
to unknown moments.

They take him aside to a beach which is empty
where the frail moonlight is resurrecting now
they stare at his face ceaselessly
unmindful of his anguish
demand from him
only a certain part of his self.

An Ode to My Granny (A True Story)

Her pain agonizingly personal—
she had encountered the marshland
the division of our lands, temples and rivers
the earth for her at that moment
extremely unreliable to live on
with apocalyptic dances of the moments of discontinuity
to go on with her journey forward
there was hardly an earthly road.

When her imagination could really take to wings
her husband
walked away as a monk to the woods.
Facing a space with white collage
she wailed
on her inescapable destiny
the riots had brought exclusion and death
freezing human relationships
obscuring the source of life
with smell of death everywhere.

Gazing on this gloom
she was quiet for some time
turned her back
against the landscape of darkness
a figure of grief
wailing for the last time.

And then . . .
began her walk to yet another land
with
only the starry night to brighten her path
the only constant part
of the syntax of her life.

A Poignant Encounter

Leaving the wilderness behind
I journey towards home
my home beside the placid lake—
When the silken chests of the blue birds
entwine clouds with their waves
leading them to strange shadowy path
I feel restless
want to hide my frivolous fear
in the cozy April warmth
bathing ceaselessly my posh pink house
with it's interlude—
my home gives me a feeling of certainty
from unknown darkness
I walk
Along the slim jade green lawn . . .
On a sudden, I feel
the earth eludes in ellipses at every step
my house pales in fear
beside the placid lake . . .
the bodies lie abruptly in the partial sunshine
my cozy little home
I find
transcendental
when the earth herself
is not so sure about her own stand
not poised anymore.

MEERA CHAKRAVORTY

Landslide: Uttaranchal

The black clouds move on
away from the mountain's embrace
in response to my poetry!
Oh no.
They past the tides of the dead over the hills
with a pompous fall of water riding over them
crushing all the frivolous claims of life
just when we faced each other
to bring that magic moment.
After waking up from the dream
the night
solitary and defeated
climbed over the clouds
to find a coherence
in it's own hollow spirit

it's long shadow is not just
some dense black dust
alive with the throbbing silence of
all who struggled
to get their voices heard—

There is love beneath these shadows
the clouds are aware
they move on
in response to my poetry
over the pompous fall of the river
past the once throbbing lives
now quiet for ever
gazing at
yet another
far away restless night.

Pretentious

Your journey will not take long
probably not much longer . . .
no, not because you are light-limbed
but intoxicated
plunged into darkness
your every step
a quick-sand journey into loveless time.

Leaving behind the green of the meadows
the trees you desire to cling to
you stop abruptly
to surrender to one you lost sight of
just then you see the maples
falling at sunset park
pale and worn out
suddenly, you feel frightened of death
go tumbling back to the tree you had left behind
the rapacious flood rushing in your breast
with no one there
in the doused streets
you throw up your arms in despair
unable to bear with the onslaughts
you wanted to make a love-life with.

Wizard's Ads . . .

Seeking attractive women 50s, early 60s
With a big heart and expansive mind
says the Ad—
The Wizard's celebrating words . . .
he can't have a thing he desires
only the words for ads
with large and changing stock of words
about his loss
his longing for his elegy
to make it alive through the
luring ads from the North
adding that
the service charges are included with the IPad
imaginatively designed
for the memorial lecture
to be held
in the bookshop across the pond.
Shrewdly,
he turns his gaze
at last
he feels no more nervous
the words will be finally
in conversation with desire
and not any more
in the company of the digital Tabs.

39
While There is Time

I will like to sit here under this Olive tree
while there is time
with my inhibitions
to pick up only those flowers
that drop into the dust
without having to be bossed into it
by the huge tree.
The wind moves on fairly briskly
carrying nostalgic tales to my rural folks
along with the stories of the golden gate
of San Francisco
about which they have no idea
in return though
they whisper the story of earth
which stopped abruptly . . .
the story of
how they stand here now
beside a new Fly-over
passing the Metro line in the city.
Earlier, in this place
there stood the gorgeous Magnolia
in full bloom
with strange legends that fascinated people.

I will like to stand here for a while
beside the Metro line
with a touch of pain
hoping that
it's deep color will reach the erstwhile Magnolia
at least now.

The Violet Chrysanthemums

40

Living in the mountains of the Dun valley
there is no remembering what flowers
grow in mist, rain and snow.
Home coming from the city that is arrogant
about supporting
long and huge calamitous buildings
which hardly breath
stuck in the dark to hide pain
I decided to take a day of rest
with glorious music to honor my presence
when a chance encounter with violet Chrysanthemums
offered a playful territory
to lead me through the wilderness
to the most strange distance
where the snow appeared meditative
detached from the image of cold and death
telling me with utter simplicity
the intricacy of an alien melody.

A Few Words

As a member of an uprooted family settled after partition on the other side of the border, I have been touched by the pain, the fear, the embarrassment, sympathy and affection of those who have walked with me.

I acknowledge the inspiration and strength derived from them in my myriad journeys, including the literary.

I deeply acknowledge the Partridge publishers for enabling this publication.